CLOUDS

Christine Webster

www.av2books.com

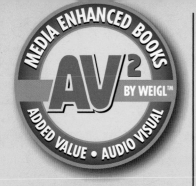

AV² provides enriched content that supplements and complements this book. Weigl's AV² books strive to create inspired learning and engage young minds in a total learning experience.

Your AV² Media Enhanced books come alive with...

 Audio
Listen to sections of the book read aloud.

 Key Words
Study vocabulary, and complete a matching word activity.

 Video
Watch informative video clips.

 Quizzes
Test your knowledge.

Go to **www.av2books.com**, and enter this book's unique code.

BOOK CODE

V698727

 Embedded Weblinks
Gain additional information for research.

 Slide Show
View images and captions, and prepare a presentation.

AV² by Weigl brings you media enhanced books that support active learning.

 Try This!
Complete activities and hands-on experiments.

... and much, much more!

Published by AV² by Weigl
350 5th Avenue, 59th Floor
New York, NY 10118
Website: www.av2books.com   www.weigl.com

Library of Congress Control Number: 2012941653
ISBN 978-1-61913-539-0 (hard cover)
ISBN 978-1-61913-541-3 (soft cover)

Printed in the United States of America in North Mankato, Minnesota
1 2 3 4 5 6 7 8 9 16 15 14 13 12

062012
WEP170512

Editor Aaron Carr
Design Ken Clarke

CONTENTS

3

Clouds have a major impact on Earth's temperature. This is because they reflect energy from the Sun back into space. Clouds can also trap heat that rises from the surface of Earth, preventing heat from escaping. Higher and thinner clouds reflect less of the Sun's energy. Lower and thicker clouds reflect more. The ability of a substance to reflect is measured by its **albedo rating**. Clouds have some of the highest albedo ratings of any natural substance.

Studying Clouds

Clouds are collections of tiny droplets of water or ice. They are important to life on this planet. They also protect Earth from too much sunshine.

Earth's atmosphere is always on the move. Great swirls of clouds dance across water and land, and then disappear. Each cloud is unique. Some are large and fluffy. Others are small and wispy. Some are white, while others are gray or black. The shape and color of a cloud tell people what kind of weather is coming.

High winds can cause clouds to move at speeds up to 100 miles (160 kilometers) per hour.

How Clouds Form

Clouds are part of the **water cycle**. Every day, the Sun heats Earth. This heat turns water from oceans, lakes, and rivers into a gas called water vapor. The water vapor then rises into the air. As it rises, it cools. The cooled water vapor **condenses** around tiny specks of dust in the air. These water droplets then crowd together to form clouds. When a cloud cannot hold any more water, it drops some of this moisture as **precipitation**. After watering the land, this moisture again fills up rivers, lakes, and oceans. Once this process is complete, the water cycle begins again.

THE WATER CYCLE

Earth's water is constantly recycled through the water cycle. No new water is created.

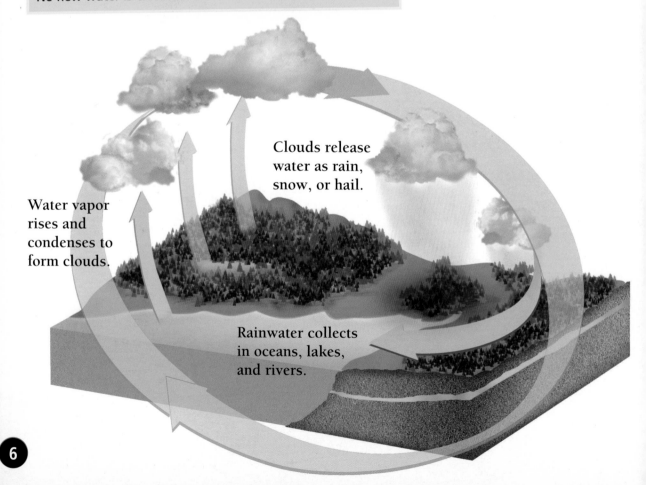

Water vapor rises and condenses to form clouds.

Clouds release water as rain, snow, or hail.

Rainwater collects in oceans, lakes, and rivers.

CLOUD COLOR

Clouds are not always white. Clouds change their color depending on the weather. On sunny days, clouds are white and fluffy. On rainy days, clouds appear thick and gray.

The color of clouds is determined by the amount of water droplets or ice crystals inside them. The droplets and crystals reflect sunlight and block it from passing through the cloud. Dark clouds contain more moisture than white clouds.

Flat, dark clouds release rain or snow. Tall, black clouds are usually a sign that stormy weather is coming. These clouds often bring lightning and thunder with them. This means a rainstorm with strong winds is on its way.

Classifying Clouds

Just like snowflakes, no two clouds are exactly alike. However, clouds can be grouped into four main types. The name of each type describes its appearance. The first type is cumulus, which means "piled up." The next type is stratus, which means "layered." Cirrus is the third type. It means "wisps of hair." The final type is nimbus, which means "rainstorm."

These names can also be combined. For example, "stratus" combined with "cumulus" make the word "stratocumulus." A stratocumulus cloud is layered and piled up. Likewise, cumulonimbus clouds are piled up clouds that produce **thunderstorms**.

■ Storm clouds bring much needed moisture to dry areas, such as inland plains.

Each type of cloud occurs at a certain height in the atmosphere.
Some clouds are high, some are low, and some occur in between.

Cirrocumulus
above 18,000 feet
(5,500 meters)

Cirrus
above 18,000 feet
(5,500 m)

Cumulonimbus
from near the ground
to above 50,000 feet
(15,000 m)

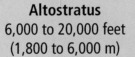

Altostratus
6,000 to 20,000 feet
(1,800 to 6,000 m)

Altocumulus
6,000 to 20,000 feet
(1,800 to 6,000 m)

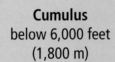

Cumulus
below 6,000 feet
(1,800 m)

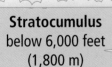

Stratocumulus
below 6,000 feet
(1,800 m)

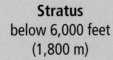

Stratus
below 6,000 feet
(1,800 m)

Cloud Types

Clouds change faster than almost any other physical feature on Earth. There are many different kinds of clouds. Each is formed by different interactions of water, heat, and wind.

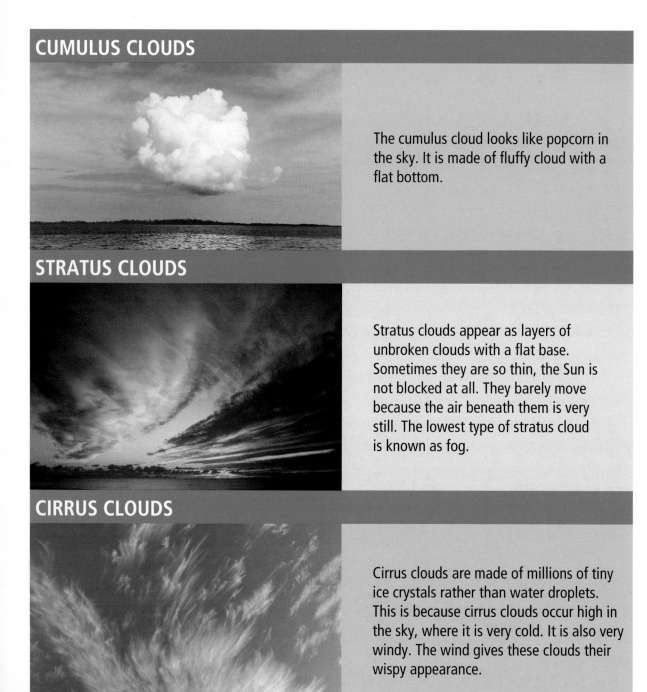

CUMULUS CLOUDS

The cumulus cloud looks like popcorn in the sky. It is made of fluffy cloud with a flat bottom.

STRATUS CLOUDS

Stratus clouds appear as layers of unbroken clouds with a flat base. Sometimes they are so thin, the Sun is not blocked at all. They barely move because the air beneath them is very still. The lowest type of stratus cloud is known as fog.

CIRRUS CLOUDS

Cirrus clouds are made of millions of tiny ice crystals rather than water droplets. This is because cirrus clouds occur high in the sky, where it is very cold. It is also very windy. The wind gives these clouds their wispy appearance.

Forecasting Weather

The type of clouds in the sky suggests what sort of weather is on the way.

| Stratus | Cumulus | Cumulonimbus | Cirrus |

Stratus clouds bring light rain or snow.

Cumulus clouds are a sign of pleasant weather.

Cumulonimbus clouds bring thunderstorms, heavy rains, snow, or hail.

Cirrus clouds are a sign that the weather is about to change.

World Wind Currents

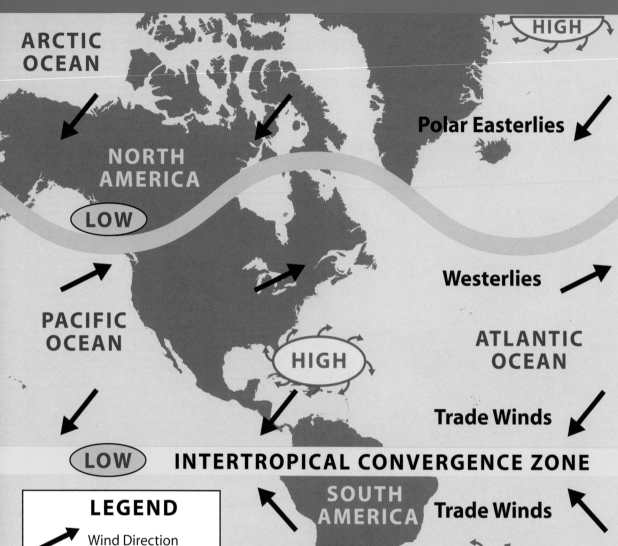

ARCTIC
OCEAN

HIGH

NORTH
AMERICA

Polar Easterlies

LOW

Westerlies

PACIFIC
OCEAN

ATLANTIC
OCEAN

HIGH

LOW

Trade Winds

INTERTROPICAL CONVERGENCE ZONE

SOUTH
AMERICA

Trade Winds

HIGH

Westerlies

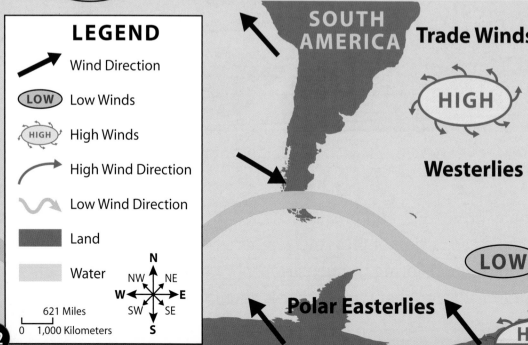

LEGEND

→ Wind Direction

LOW Low Winds

HIGH High Winds

⤴ High Wind Direction

〰 Low Wind Direction

■ Land

■ Water

621 Miles
0   1,000 Kilometers

N
NW NE
W ✦ E
SW SE
S

LOW

Polar Easterlies

HIGH

Cloud Seeding

Earth needs moisture. Sometimes, an area does not receive enough moisture. A cloud passing over such an area can be seeded with special particles to make it rain. This is called cloud seeding.

For a cloud to release rain, tiny water droplets must join together to form bigger, heavier drops of water. Natural raindrops form when water vapor condenses on dust or salt in the air. Cloud seeding provides the specks on which the droplets form. A chemical called silver iodide is released into the cloud from attachments on the wings of an airplane. Moisture clings to the particles of silver iodide and falls as rain. Silver iodide may also prevent large hailstones from forming and destroying farmers' crops.

■ Aircraft must be fitted with special equipment to release silver iodide into clouds.

Pollution and Clouds

Not all clouds are gentle and fluffy. Some clouds are filled with harmful chemicals. Smoke from fires and factories adds chemicals to the air, as does exhaust from cars and trucks. In large amounts, these chemicals can harm the environment. They can create **air pollution**. Water vapor in the air can cling to these chemicals and form clouds. Water in these clouds becomes polluted. This polluted water falls to the ground as **acid rain**. Acid rain can **corrode** buildings and statues. It can even kill plants and poison drinking water.

■ Factories, mills, and power stations release billions of pounds (kilograms) of pollution into Earth's atmosphere every year.

What is an Atmospheric Scientist?

Atmospheric scientists study the physical properties of the atmosphere. They learn how clouds form in different situations. They also observe how changes in the atmosphere can affect the weather we experience every day.

These scientists do not only study Earth's atmosphere. Other planets have clouds and storms as well. Atmospheric scientists use other planets as models. This helps them understand how Earth's atmosphere will behave under different conditions.

Anthony Del Genio

Dr. Anthony Del Genio works at the NASA Goddard Institute for Space Studies. He studies clouds to forecast how the climate might change in the future. Dr. Del Genio examines weather conditions by using information from satellites and from instruments on Earth. He also studies weather conditions on other planets.

Scientists use computers, satellites, and radar to study clouds.

Seven Facts About Clouds

Some storm clouds release as much energy as an **atomic bomb**.

Fog is a type of cloud that hangs at ground level.

On most days, more than half of Earth's surface is covered by clouds.

The patterns of light and dark stripes seen on Jupiter are caused by different types of clouds.

Cirrus clouds are sometimes called "mare's tails" for their wispy appearance.

Snow and rain falling from clouds create all of Earth's glaciers and feed nearly all of its rivers and lakes.

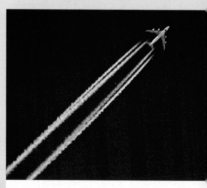

Airplanes can make their own clouds. They are formed from water vapor that is pushed out of the plane's engine.

Cloud Brain Teasers

1   Name three forms of precipitation.

2   What type of clouds look like wisps of hair?

3   What type of cloud is a sign that a storm is coming?

4   Why are clouds sometimes seeded?

5   What are clouds made of?

6   Why are some clouds darker than others?

7   What is fog?

8   Name three things clouds do for Earth.

9   Why do people hear thunder after they see the lightning?

10   What is an atmospheric scientist?

ANSWERS: 1. Rain, snow, or hail **2.** Cirrus clouds **3.** Cumulonimbus clouds **4.** To force a cloud to release rain **5.** Ice crystals or water droplets **6.** Because they have more water droplets or ice crystals in them **7.** A cloud that hangs at ground level **8.** Clouds carry water and drop it on dry land. They protect Earth from too much sunshine. They keep warmth near the surface of the planet. **9.** Because light travels faster than sound **10.** A scientist who studies clouds and the atmosphere

Science in Action

Become a Junior Atmospheric Scientist

This activity can be done alone or with an adult.

Materials Needed

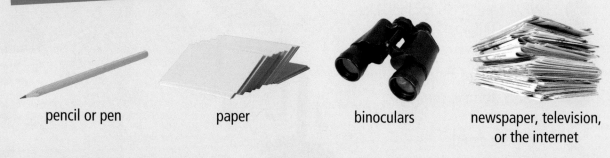

pencil or pen   paper   binoculars   newspaper, television, or the internet

Directions

1 Take some time to observe the sky every day for one week. Write down the types of clouds that you see.

2 Using local news from a newspaper, the television, the radio, or the internet, record the temperature and rainfall for each day. Write this next to the cloud types you recorded.

3 Using the chart of cloud types found in this book, try to identify the clouds you see. Do you see a connection between the type of cloud observed and the weather on a given day?

Key Words

acid rain: rain that has become a weak acid by mixing with pollution in the air

air pollution: harmful materials, such as gases and chemicals, that pollute the air

albedo rating: measurement of the amount of light absorbed by a surface

astronomer: scientists who study outer space, planets, and the universe

atmospheric scientist: someone who studies Earth's atmosphere

atomic bomb: a bomb that causes a huge explosion

carbon dioxide: a colorless, odorless gas

condenses: changes from a gas to a liquid by cooling

corrode: dissolve or wear away

precipitation: moisture released from clouds as rain, snow, or hail

thunderstorms: storms that usually feature thunder, lightning, and heavy precipitation

water cycle: the process by which all of Earth's water is recycled

Index

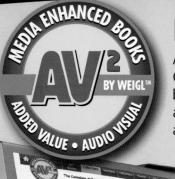

Log on to www.av2books.com

AV[2] by Weigl brings you media enhanced books that support active learning. Go to www.av2books.com, and enter the special code found on page 2 of this book. You will gain access to enriched and enhanced content that supplements and complements this book. Content includes video, audio, weblinks, quizzes, a slide show, and activities.

Audio
Listen to sections of the book read aloud.

Video
Watch informative video clips.

Embedded Weblinks
Gain additional information for research.

Try This!
Complete activities and hands-on experiments.

WHAT'S ONLINE?

Try This!	Embedded Weblinks	Video	EXTRA FEATURES
Complete a water cycle activity.	Learn more about clouds.	Watch a video about the types of clouds.	**Audio** Listen to sections of the book read aloud.
Identify the types of clouds.	Find weather forecasts for your area.	Watch a video about storm clouds.	
Try a wind current mapping activity.	Read more about the water cycle.		**Key Words** Study vocabulary, and complete a matching word activity.
Test your knowledge of clouds.	Learn more about how storm clouds form.		
			Slide Show View images and captions, and prepare a presentation
			Quizzes Test your knowledge.

AV[2] was built to bridge the gap between print and digital. We encourage you to tell us what you like and what you want to see in the future.

Sign up to be an AV[2] Ambassador at www.av2books.com/ambassador.

THE BEAR
WHO HAD NO PLACE
TO GO

by James Stevenson

HARPER & ROW, PUBLISHERS
New York, Evanston, San Francisco, London

Library of Congress Catalog Card Number: 70-186775
Trade Standard Book Number: 06-025780-6
Harpercrest Standard Book Number: 06-025781-4

Format by Kohar Alexanian

CHAPTERS

Without a Job

Ralph was a bear who rode a bicycle in the circus. When the circus band played, Ralph went around and around the ring on his bike.

Everybody loved to see Ralph ride, especially when he did "no hands." The crowd clapped and cheered. Ralph was very proud.

Ralph liked almost everything about the circus. But after the last show, the crowds went home, and the other animals were put into their cages. Ralph would watch the roustabouts take down the big tent in the moonlight, and he would feel all alone.

Late at night he would ride on the special circus train
to the next town. And before he went to sleep, Ralph
would look at the country going by.

Then he would get into his striped pajamas, climb into his berth, listen to the wheels of the train clacking, and watch the stars until he fell asleep.

One day, Mr. Doll, who was the boss of the circus, said to Ralph, "I have bad news for you, kid. You have been a terrific bicycle-rider, but the circus needs a new act. I have hired a seal who can play 'Stars and Stripes Forever' on horns, and this seal is taking your place."

"Taking my place?" said Ralph.

"Yeah," said Mr. Doll. "We can't use you anymore. Sorry, Ralph."

Ralph couldn't believe it. The circus was the only life he knew.

"You can keep the bike, Ralph," said Mr. Doll. "Good luck."

That night, after
the show was over,
Ralph went around
and said good-bye to
all the circus people
and animals.

For the last time he watched the roustabouts take
down the tent and put everything on the train. Then,
when the whole circus was aboard—except for Ralph—
the whistle tooted, and Ralph watched the train go
away without him.

After a while, Ralph put on his pajamas and tried to
go to sleep, but it was hard to sleep without the sound
of train wheels clacking. It was very quiet. It was too
quiet, and too dark, and much too lonely.

When Ralph woke up it was morning. Nobody was around. He decided to get on his bike and find some-place where there were people, and things happening. He put his pajamas on the bicycle seat, and started off.

On the Road

Soon Ralph came to a big highway. There were lots of cars and trucks, and they were all going very fast. A sign said TO THE CITY. Everybody honked their horns at Ralph because he wasn't going fast enough, and a lot of people glared at him. Ralph pedaled faster.

14

When he finally got to the city, Ralph didn't know what to do. All the people were walking very fast. Nobody said hello. It was noisy and hot. Ralph sat down in the shade to think.

The people kept rushing by. It was like the crowd coming to the circus, but there were no children, and nobody was laughing.

Ralph decided to get out of the city and look for a small town. The highway went through a lot of places that were smoky and smelly. After a while, Ralph came to a small town that looked okay.

16

Ralph decided he would try to get a job. He went into
a grocery store and told the man that he would like to
deliver groceries on his bicycle.

"How could you carry them?" asked the man.

"I happen to be able to ride with no hands," said
Ralph.

"Let's see," said the man.

Ralph picked up a box of groceries and got on his
bike and started to ride.

"Not bad," said the man. "Take them to the yellow
house at the end of the street."

Ralph was doing fine when suddenly an old circus poster caught his eye. He forgot where he was and what he was doing—all Ralph could think of was the circus. He could almost hear the band, and smell the popcorn, and then—

Ralph crashed into a policeman who was standing on
the corner. The groceries went flying.

"I'm very sorry," said Ralph. "I was delivering these groceries."

The policeman stared at him.

Then the grocer ran up.

"Does this bear work for you?" asked the policeman.

"Not any more, Officer," said the grocer.

Ralph picked up the groceries and gave them to the
man, and said he was sorry again. Then he got on his
bike and rode out of town into the country.

Ralph was feeling very sad and lonely. Then it started to rain. As he came to the top of a hill, he saw a rat hitchhiking at the side of the road. The rat looked very wet.

Ralph stopped. "Want a lift?" he asked.

"Sure do," said the rat. "Thanks." He climbed onto the handlebars. "Where did you find the cool bike?" he asked.

"I used to be in the circus," said Ralph, starting to pedal.

"The *circus*?" said the rat. "Wow! It's a pleasure to meet a famous performer. My name's Frank."

"I'm Ralph," said Ralph.

"How come you left the circus?" said Frank. "Got tired of all the bright lights and excitement, I suppose?"

"No. I got replaced by a seal," said Ralph.

"A seal on a bicycle?" said Frank. "That's some act! Wow!"

"No. He played horns," said Ralph.

"No kidding," said Frank. "Where are you headed now?"

"I don't know exactly," said Ralph. "Where are *you* going?"

"To the woods—want to come along?" said Frank.

"Sure," said Ralph. "What's the woods?"

"Oh, it's cool," said Frank. "Big trees, wild stuff, plants with berries—the whole thing. No people, and lots of animals. A nice crowd."

"Sounds good," said Ralph. "Which way?"

"Just keep pedaling," said Frank.

After a couple of hours, they had left the last town far behind, and the sun was coming out. Ralph was getting tired, but Frank kept saying, "Straight ahead, we're almost there!"

"This is it," said Frank when they came to the woods
at last. "What do you think?"

"It looks okay," said Ralph.

"Let's go," said Frank.

The Woods

Ralph and Frank walked into the woods, and it was beautiful, but Ralph didn't see any animals. "Where is everybody?" he asked.

"Oh, they're around," said Frank. He knocked on a hollow tree.

"Yes?" said a voice.

"Stick your head out and say hello to my pal Ralph," called Frank.

A moment later, a raccoon peered out. "How do you do?" he said.

"Hi," said Ralph.

"Ralph's going to be with us for a while," said Frank.

"Splendid," said the raccoon.

Then Frank introduced Ralph to a deer who was standing nearby. Ralph had not even noticed the deer, because she stood so quietly.

Frank and Ralph walked farther into the woods.

"These are the opossums, directly overhead," said Frank.

"Hello," said Ralph.

"Welcome to the woods," said the opossums.

"Don't step on the turtle," said Frank.

"How do you do?" said Ralph.

"Pleased to meet you," said the turtle.

Pretty soon, Ralph was saying hello to all sorts of
animals—a skunk, a chipmunk, an owl, a beaver, a frog.
Everyone was friendly.

Then Frank introduced
Ralph to two bears. "Meet
Herb and Paul," he said.

"Hi," said Ralph.

"It's always good to see a
new bear," said Herb.

"Welcome," said Paul.

A lot of the animals gathered around and asked Ralph to tell them about the circus. Ralph told all about the acrobats and the clowns and the elephants and the band and the popcorn and the roustabouts and the train.

Then the animals asked him to do his act, so Ralph showed how he rode his bike. All the animals said he was very good.

The next day Ralph and Frank
played with the bears. Herb and Paul
showed Ralph how to climb trees.

They showed him a
good place to go swim-
ming too. Ralph had a
wonderful time.

One day in November, when the wind was blowing the last few leaves off the trees, Ralph hurried to play with Herb and Paul as usual.

"Hey," said Ralph. "What do you want to do today?"

"Nothing," said Herb. "We're all through for this year. We're going to hibernate now."

"Hibernate?" said Ralph.

"Sure," said Herb. "Don't *you* hibernate?"

"I don't know," said Ralph. "What is it?"

"We go to sleep for the winter," said Herb.

"You really sleep for the whole winter?" said Ralph.

"Bears always sleep for the winter," said Herb.

"Every year," said Paul. "Then, in the spring, we wake up and go out, and it's really great."

"Oh," said Ralph.

"You want us to show you a good cave to hibernate in?" asked Paul.

"No, thanks," said Ralph. "I couldn't possibly sleep all winter."

"Well, too bad, Ralph," said Herb. "There won't be much doing around here for the next few months. Just a lot of snow and ice and cold wind."

Ralph began to feel very lonely. "I guess I'll leave the woods," he said. "Go someplace else."

But Ralph knew there was no place else to go.

Ralph looked at his bike. A few snowflakes fell, and
the air was cold. He walked around the woods, taking
a last look at everything—the trees he had played in
with Herb and Paul, the place where they swam.

Ralph was sitting against a tree when the skunk came along.

"Hey, Ralph," said the skunk. "You going to be sitting here for a minute?"

"I guess so," said Ralph.

"Good," said the skunk. "Don't move."

The skunk disappeared for a few minutes. Ralph could hear some of the animals talking. He heard Frank saying, "Quiet, everybody—quiet!"

And he heard the owl hoot. He couldn't figure out what was going on. Then the skunk came back.

The skunk climbed on a rock and said, "We have a surprise for you, Ralph. We are now going to present the Big Woods Circus!"

As Ralph watched, the beaver ran out and did a juggling act with acorns.

The possums swung from a tree branch while the frog, the woodpecker, and the owl made music.

Herb and Paul did a clown act, tripping and falling down a lot.

Frank did a balancing act with the turtle and the chipmunk.

The deer ran out with two raccoons on her back.

The squirrels did an act flying through the air, high up in the trees.

Afterward, all the animals came out and bowed. Ralph clapped and clapped.

"It was as good as the other circus," said Ralph. "Maybe even better."

Frank said, "We did the circus for you because we want you to stay in the woods with us. Everybody likes you, and we don't want you to leave. We want to do another circus next year with you as the star, showing us how. Then maybe we could put it on for the other animals over on Black Mountain."

"Will you stay?" asked the chipmunk.
"Will you?" said the skunk.
"How about it?" said Paul.
Ralph smiled. "Okay," he said.
Everybody cheered.

"I picked you out a cave, just in case," said Frank.
He took Ralph to a cave on the side of a hill.
"There it is," said Frank. "Nice and quiet."
Ralph went in and took a look around.

"Perfect place to hibernate," said Frank. "Very restful." Then he added, "I put your pajamas there, just in case..."

"Thanks, Frank," said Ralph. "I'll give it a try." He put on his pajamas.

Frank said he'd be back in a minute—he wanted to go get an acorn or two.

The leaves were really comfortable. Ralph thought about his new friends and his new life in the woods. He began to get sleepy. He imagined what it would be like in the spring.

By the time Frank got back a few minutes later,
Ralph was sound asleep.

Ralph slept all winter long.

And when he finally woke up—

it was spring, and he could hear Herb and Paul and
everybody already playing in the woods.

"Wait for me, everybody—I just woke up!" Ralph
yelled. "Wait for me!"
And he ran, as fast as he could, to join them.

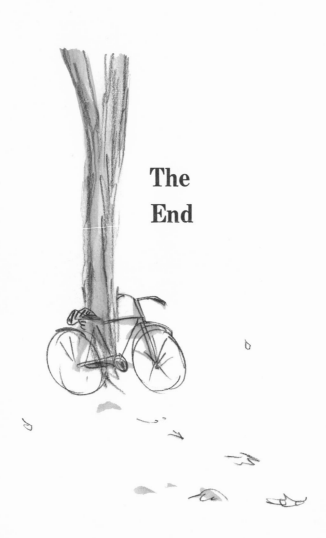

The
End

E
S

Stevenson, James

The bear who had no
place to go

DATE			
MAR 1 APR 5			
APR 4			
OCT 2 9 1980			
MAY 2 1981			
OCT 2 1 1982 APR			
APR			

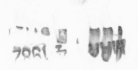

© THE BAKER & TAYLOR CO.